I0439455

Don't Fluck It Up

The Perfect YOU for the Job Interview

Aimee Corinne Tittlemier

Don't Fluck It Up
Copyright © 2014 by Aimee Corinne Tittlemier

ISBN-13: 978-1497463455

Printed in USA by Create Space, an Amazon Company

Table of Contents

PREFACE:
KNOCK ON EVERY DOOR AND SEE WHICH ONES OPEN

***

Searching for a job and career that is meant for you can be a tedious process, especially in a time when the economy makes for an overly competitive job market. At times, you may feel exhausted from searching for jobs, applying for multiple positions, facing judgment and rejection, and picking yourself up to start the process over again.

Though you cannot control whom a company ends up hiring, you can absolutely make sure that you *Don't Fluck It Up* and secure your position as one of the top candidates. By having the right tools, you can strengthen and multiply your chances of being hired into a position that compliments your personal set of skills. Once you have the tools, it is up to you to tailor, practice and perfect your application and interview techniques, becoming a notable competitor and candidate for any position. The hiring process is a huge opportunity to begin your career, or to start a new career path.

Life is full of opportunity and it would be a shame not to enjoy and partake in the things that are offered to you. Sometimes the best opportunities are the ones that are unexpected, or the ones that seem complex and confusing.

INTRODUCTION
A LITTLE ABOUT ME

***

It was so much easier to imagine myself in a career when I was younger. Of course, I wanted to play for the Dallas Cowboys, while being a radio host, teacher and a Broadway star all in one lifetime…and it didn't seem unreachable back then. Every day I had a different profession and would use my little sister and stuffed animals to make the job come to life. We even used to print pictures of food off of the computer and design menus for the grand opening of our restaurant (which got rave reviews). Anything and everything was possible.

At a very young age I was active in academics. I would participate in most school contests such as the spelling bees, the science fairs, track meets and even oral language competitions. Throughout elementary school, I always took home a high award for my efforts and would be disappointed if I didn't finish in the top three.

I spent my high school years preparing for college, racking up all the extracurricular activities and exhausting myself for one more academic award. I made sure I was a part of every campus club (even The League of Extraordinary Gentlemen) and was even elected as the Student Body Vice President.

I was accepted into Loyola Marymount University in Los Angeles, California as a theater major, as I loved the stage and all the aspects of putting on a production. After the first half of the semester, I realized that it was not the right fit for me. I did not want to skate through college trying to make myself cry on cue, while getting rejected by the industry for being me. I wasn't interested in being told what I physically needed to change to 'fit' the role and instead decided this career path was not for me.

I had to take a creative writing class for core curriculum credits and ended up falling in love with the art of writing. We were free to break all the rules of writing and tell stories the way we wanted to tell them. I was able to express myself with delicious words that would drip from my lips and take others with me to places that only existed in my mind. I studied classic and modern writing from all areas of the world, and then further studied the authors and what inspired them, scared them, or altered their world to see through different eyes. I dabbled in poetry, fiction writing and journalism – any class I could enroll in to teach me more about communicating through the written word.

In my junior year, I thought I had found what I wanted to do for a career and decided to start working for the school newspaper. I imagined I would be writing articles that would challenge the thinking of the school and its students, but instead I was assigned the job of reviewing plays of our theater department. At first, I took the job with determination that I would pay my dues and then move up to the more socially and politically important topics. After my creatively critical review came back to me with red slashes all over it, I turned it in with the corrections for print along with my resignation. I did not want to work in a position where someone dictated each word to my typing fingers.

With all those years of preparation for the working world and graduating with honors from a prestigious university, I then found myself back at Mom and Dad's house asking myself the inevitable question—what did I want to do with my life?

Now, there were plenty of inspirational self-help books that were available to assist me in 'seeking the right career,' or 'finding myself,' but even if they pointed me in the right direction, I felt as though I would be wasting my time reading books instead of applying for jobs. (One of the reasons this book is a quick read). Unfortunately, reading would not bring in the rent check.

I'm the type that needs instant gratification, so I jumped into any position I could find. This meant working a few jobs that weren't ideal before finding where I belonged. Looking back, I can confidently say that I wouldn't change the path I took to find my best-fit career. By experiencing the types of positions that I enjoyed and even the ones that I did not fit, I was able to narrow the huge amount of employment fields. Even the unfavorable positions gave me valuable lessons or experience that I might not have gained otherwise. My parents always encouraged me to be my own best advocate, and in doing so, created a strong-willed woman who dug my own path career path by putting myself out there, lots of prayer and preparation, and seeing where life would lead me next.

Now, I humbly offer my experiences and knowledge to you in hopes that you can be encouraged to find your own career.

Chapter One
THE "UNEMPLOYMENT" JOB DESCRIPTION

***

In this economy, it is seemingly difficult to find *any* job, let alone a career. Surprisingly, though, the job market has an abundance of open positions awaiting applicants. If unemployed, your job is to apply to as many open positions as possible. Make it a point to work full-time searching through job openings and submitting your application. This is your opportunity to start a new path in life; view this opportunity as a chance to start over and try any profession you've ever wondered about working.

Join a Job Posting Website

There are many job websites out there available free of

charge. Some of my favorites are www.monster.com or www.careerbuilder.com, though there is an unlimited number. Most sites have the same postings, so signing up for one or two is sufficient. There are also job sites devoted to specific industries. www.malakye.com focuses on job postings within the action sports industry, making it easier for employers and job seekers with the same interests and talents to be united. If you have a specific company in mind that you'd like to apply for, you should go directly to their website to see the available openings and application process.

Take the time to set up a strong profile for yourself and be open to different job categories that you haven't yet explored. You should look at any job openings that sound interesting to you; even if you don't have all the skills or experience the employers are looking for in an applicant. The more doors you prop open, the more opportunities you create for yourself.

Set a Daily Application Goal

Every day, get your cup of coffee, a hearty breakfast, get dressed and head off to your office (even if that's just your couch). Don't let yourself lounge in your pajamas or sweatpants, as your attire will reflect your attitude. Set yourself up to be confident, aggressive and successful in your search for a job.

Set a daily goal for getting out applications. Remember, your full-time job is searching for openings and applying for positions, so set the goal high to fill your workday. Again, apply for any and all positions that intrigue you or capture your attention. Commit your allotted "work" time to searching and applying for jobs, but after the work day is done, take a rest.

Continue or pick up some hobbies that will take your mind away from the application process, if only for a few hours. Attend your cardio or yoga classes regularly, go on a bike ride, walk your dog, or even pick up a skill like knitting. All these extra activities will continue to challenge your mind, help you to maintain a healthy lifestyle and clear your head to start fresh the next day.

Now take into consideration the specific set of skills that you have. Many postings will have specifications or requirements for the applicant, such as a certain certificate or degree needed. These requirements are set for the applicants because they are non-negotiable for the job being offered. Focus on your own areas of talent and apply to positions that you believe you can confidently offer to employers and you will find that your preference of positions will begin to narrow. This is not to say that you shouldn't branch out to explore other openings, but to apply for a physician position without a medical degree is just a waste of time.

After a while, it becomes exciting to get on the websites and see what new positions have opened. Routinely applying for new job openings not only puts yourself out to potential employers, but also helps you to learn what your strengths are and how you can personally contribute to different positions.

Sometimes it helps to create a work atmosphere for yourself rather than sitting at home. Drive to your local coffeehouse and set up your workspace at one of their tables. This forces you to have an acceptable appearance, a more focused mindset, and a determination to get your work done (all while having the added bonus of a delicious mocha latte).

Use All Resources

While applying for positions online is quick and successful, make sure you are exercising all of your resources for finding open positions. Look in the local newspaper, network with family and friends, and visit local job fairs. You can always walk into a business that you are interested in working for and inquire about any open positions. It is *okay* to be more aggressive when looking for a job. This economy makes for an extremely competitive environment and your initiative to be a strong voice for yourself will only better your chances at landing that interview or job.

Two of my past positions were found by reaching out to my family and friends to let them know I was looking for a job. In one case, my sister received an email from a manager of a company she had interned for in college. He was looking to fill an entry-level position and was asking for referrals from his database, which contained all of his clients, friends and employees, past and present. I had no prior experience in the industry, but was eager to learn.

The brief introduction from my sister, followed by sending in a well-written cover letter and resume highlighting my skills that paralleled the position description landed me the interview. My enthusiasm and determination landed me the job. Coincidentally, while I was at the same company another position opened and the manager again, reached out to his database for referrals. Make sure your friends and family know you're looking – those connections can lead to golden job opportunities.

Lastly, don't be afraid to start in an entry-level position. An entry-level position is a great way to start with a company and demonstrate your set of skills. Learn the business by asking questions and taking on all responsibilities that are offered. As you establish your value at the company, you will easily start to climb the ladder of promotion.

Don't Lose Heart

The best thing to keep in mind is that you are not the only one going through this process. I set expectations for myself to finish college, land a solid career and begin my adult life all within a matter of a couple years. The one thing that surprised me the most about being home with my parents was how many other people my age were home with their parents too. Know that it is a more competitive environment to find and, harder yet, *keep* a job, but use that information as motivation to be the best competitor.

Remember that you do not have to land a job that will be your long-term career on your first try. Experiencing different jobs is a great way to find out what you do and don't want in a career, as well as open more avenues to other prospective jobs. The career comes when you are happy with the company you are working for and you are the perfect piece to complete the puzzle of the company. Everyone has something special to contribute; you just have to find where your contribution is most needed.

While I was back in my parents' home, looking for a job, I was also working three part time jobs to keep my morale high. It can become exhausting to sit in front of a computer all day without seeing quick results. I taught exercise classes, dance classes, and became a substitute teacher for the local elementary to high school districts. Make sure to keep your free time occupied so that your mind and body stay active and you have a fresh start each day. You can even network through the customers and co-workers in your part-time positions. Don't allow yourself to become lazy. You are your best advocate.

It's Okay to Be Picky

Even though this economy presents a tough and competitive job market, that doesn't mean that you have to settle for any job that will accept you. Ideally, you want to end up in a position that you can be proud working. You want a position that motivates you to get up every morning and to work towards a larger goal. Be picky with the applications you choose to send. Send as many as you can, but make sure if you are called for an interview that you can see yourself as a part of that company. Choosing to send applications to positions, that you would turn down anyway, only wastes your time as well as the employer's time.

Of course, we all need the paycheck, but it is not worth draining yourself mentally, physically or emotionally just to pay the rent; you'll find you are working an undesirable job just to live in a mediocre place with barely enough free time to enjoy your life. Your energy will be diminished and you'll be too tired to even try branching out with new hobbies.

My best example of the wrong position was working for a company while living in Los Angeles. Living near the Venice and Santa Monica beaches sounded relaxing since I loved lying in the sand and even getting a surf session in every once in a while. The job was so draining and I was so unhappy with my position that I never once made it to the sand while I worked there. Defeated and deflated after every workday, I drove home through Los Angeles traffic and never found the time to experience all the fun elements of the grand city.

Chapter Two
ONLY ONE FIRST IMPRESSION

***

I've been on both sides of the resume. I've had to compose attention-grabbing attributes about myself on a piece of paper and hope that my words synchronized with some employer's ideal candidate for the open position. I've also had the responsibility of shuffling through hundreds of resumes to find a few that fit my job description. The truth is that each employer is looking for key words within their stack of resumes that correspond to the position they are looking to fill. Unfortunately, many of the resumes get one glance and then are thrown into the recycling bin. You only get one quick chance to clearly and positively represent yourself as an amazing applicant.

I've seen all kinds of resumes that try to grab attention in obnoxiously obvious ways: printing on thick cardstock paper, colored paper, glossy paper and any other type of paper imaginable. I've received electronic resumes with highlighted sections and underlined attributes. I've even received a resume in an e-card before. Though it might have brought a fleeting smile to my face, all of those resumes were quickly discarded. I was looking for a serious candidate for the position I had to offer. The way the resume is presented is like a first interview. You want to show up looking professional and ready to work, not show up in a comical outfit that makes the employer question your sincerity.

The resume itself should be a simple, yet elegant document. It needs to show professionalism in presentation, while remaining straightforward in content. Too simplistic and lacking in detail will represent a candidate that might be too elementary for the position. Too much detail will leave nothing to the imagination and overwhelm the reviewer. You want to give just enough detail to make the employer want to pull you in for an interview and ask questions about the points listed on your resume.

Formatting the Resume—Learning to Let Go

Your resume should not be more than one page. Period. I know you are much more amazing than can be contained in one page, but learn to let go of unnecessary information. List only the most prevalent key points under each company in your employment history, consolidating your job responsibilities and achievements. You should list a maximum of four companies in your employment experience.

Though this might seem like a simple task, it is one of the things people struggle with most when compiling their resumes. Edit, edit, edit. It is acceptable to adjust the margins a bit and even adjust the font size, but cut out the excess. If you cannot decide what to cut out, have someone else take a look at your resume to advise what parts are excessive. With the help of others' eyes, you can separate the facts from the fluff.

As you learn to let go, you can also learn to add more important attributes when you gain additional skills. Be a continual learner by taking comprehension classes on the latest business software, become familiar with Microsoft

Office and the updates that have been made to those programs commonly used in the professional environment. As you gain more knowledge, highlight it on your resume and let go of a different skill that might be more outdated.

Highlight Your Attributes – Use Your Words

Growing up, whenever I was mad or frustrated, my mom would tell me to 'use my words,' encouraging me to find a way to express myself that was more meaningful and complex than just letting her know that I was mad. She wanted to know how I felt and what was driving my anger, rather than hearing any meaningless curse words spill from my lips.

In the same way, your resume should use expressive words that accentuate your abilities. My best friend and computer homepage is www.thesaurus.com, where you can find many ways to say the same word. Some word choices reach further or sound more professional than others. The key is to select the words that contribute most to the highlighting of your attributes.

The thesaurus can also prevent you from sounding too repetitive when listing the key responsibilities of your selected positions. Avoid being the "one-word-wonder" when showcasing the variety of skills and responsibilities you've acquired.

Under your additional skills section, list those attributes that best pertain to the job description. Include the different computer and software programs in which you are proficient, as well as any other special attributes that increase your value as a candidate. For general resume purposes, it is best to list all business related skills, but ideally you will contour your resume for each application. See that your resume parallels what the employer is asking for in an applicant. For example, if the position calls for marketing responsibilities, choose past positions you've held that reflect marketing assignments or similar business.

Do not lie on your resume. Too much exaggeration will hurt you later in the hiring process. Though it might make you look better on paper, lying won't get you past the first interview. Interviewers use your resume to create questions that delve further into your work history. If the interviewer finds that you have misrepresented yourself, there will be a negative view of you as a potential applicant. No employer is going to want to risk hiring anyone who is dishonest.

Your best plan of attack is to be completely honest about your work history and acquired skills. Lying on your resume is only wasting everyone's time. Instead of exaggerating, become an expert at wording your job responsibilities and experiences in a way that sounds more professional.

Examples:

Instead of – Filing Client Reports

Try – Organized Client Files and Reports

Instead of – Answered phones and emails

Try – Provided superb customer service by answering questions and inquiries via phone and email

Instead of – Cleaned the bar area

Try – Maintained an immaculate workspace

By using a more colorful and sophisticated vocabulary, you are using the art of telling the truth. The resume should be a work of art or a compellation of elegant words that best represent you.

You don't have to be fully chronological with your job history, but if you are missing a length of time between jobs, be prepared to answer why there is a gap in your work history. Life happens. When I was creating my resume, I had a few jobs that lasted for a year or less, but felt as though I gained important experience from those particular positions. Some of jobs ended due to the economical and budget cuts, and others ended because I found better opportunities. I decided to list them on my resume because I knew that I had made an impression at the companies I worked with even if it was in a short amount of time.

Employers are knowledgeable of the current economy. They are aware that it is difficult to hold down a job in this market and will not usually be judgmental of short employment gaps. Again, you might be asked to explain the gap, but do not be embarrassed to say you were looking for employment during that time. It is honorable to put yourself out there for employment, as well as being honest about your efforts.

Be certain if you list a past job on your resume that you have a positive relationship with that particular employer. It's amazing how many people share a network, and the employer is going to use all of their resources to find out more about you. If you left any company with a negative impression, do not list them on your resume.

While looking to hire for an assistant position, I met with a candidate that seemed desirable, but when I contacted one of the previous employers, I got a mediocre assessment of the person, highlighting a pedestrian work ethic when I was looking for someone who would go above and beyond all expectations. Had it not been for the inferior report from the past employer, the candidate might have had a better chance at the position. Any of your previous positions on your resume should come with an employer that would write a raving reference letter for your character and work ethic. Sometimes it's not possible to get raving reviews from every employer, but at least leave each position with a positive impression so no harsh words can be said to harm your chances at another position.

Occasionally, exceptions may occur. A personal risk I took on my own resume building process was to list a job position that I held for one month. In this case, I left the company amicably, but I'm sure the employer wouldn't have had much to say about my work ethic since they had no time to make an assessment. The reason I decided to display this position on my resume was to create a question for the employer to ask. I wanted to highlight that I left the company because it was not a fit for me. It was important for me to express my belief that a person has to fit the specific work environment, and if it is not a fit, it can be counterproductive to all parties. I don't suggesting taking risks on your resume unless you are confident that you can portray these risks in a confident way.

Formatting – Use Your Space

You want your resume to take up a full page. Even if you don't have much work history, create a document that is full of information. Again, this is your first impression for the potential employers. Leave them wanting to invite you for an interview. There are many types of resume formats to use. You can find multiple formats of resumes on the

Internet, all of which are acceptable. Find a format that looks professional to you and use it as a guide to create your own resume. Take the format and make it your own, personalize and customize it to represent yourself.

For one of my resumes, I used a simple and clean format that allowed me to share my academic achievements as well as my work history, and special skills. The education section allowed me to showcase my prestigious study efforts, but also allowed for my page to be filled. During school, I worked side jobs as a coffee barista, math tutor, dance teacher and aerobics instructor, but once I entered the professional world, I wanted my resume to reflect the job positions that were most relevant to the positions for which I was applying. By choosing a template that allowed me to highlight education and specific skills, while listing the three most applicable positions, I was able to submit a competitive resume.

Tailor your resume to correlate with the job descriptions of any open positions. If the potential job wants someone with many managerial qualities and experience in customer service, make sure your job history touches on past positions that would demonstrate those traits.

Help and Revision

When you've finished writing your resume, at the very least make sure to hit the spell check button. It is imperative that your resume does not have any grammatical errors on it.

When I receive an abundance of resumes for a job opening, my first way of narrowing down candidates is by eliminating any applicant that has grammatical errors on the documents they submitted. Your resume is the most important document when you are looking for employment and if you submit it with errors, the employer will already assume that you are not detail oriented and are careless with communication—two characteristics that are detrimental to your application.

It is always a good idea to have another person look over your resume. You can use your school career center, a trusted teacher, or a professional acquaintance. It is just healthy for your ego to have a second pair of eyes look over your work for constructive revisions or opinions on how to improve and strengthen your resume. Often times, being human, we get so wrapped up in the pride of creating a masterpiece that we fail to see all the flaws.

Continuously revise and rewrite your resume as you gain more work experience, acquire more professional knowledge, or earn more achievements. Potential employers want to see your most recent qualifications and how you've continued to better yourself.

Chapter Three
COVER LETTER – YOUR GRAND ENTRANCE

***

One thing sorely lacking in the many resumes I've received is a cover letter. Your cover letter is your introduction, or your *grande entrée*. It is a way for you to give the potential employer a taste of who you are as a person. You've put together an impressive professional document that gives the employer an idea of your work ethic and experience, but this is your chance to explain why you want or deserve the position.

You want to write the cover letter with professionalism, but also find a way to make yourself stand out from the rest of the resumes. While you can also find generic templates for cover letters with a simple Google search, keep in mind that the templates are so general that anyone can plug their information in and use them. The goal of your cover letter is to give the employer a glimpse into your personality. You could start the cover letter with a favorite quote that is applicable to the position, or a shocking statement that intrigues the reader. Think of a creative way to catch your reader's attention.

Employers like to see cover letters because offices have certain dynamics. If you are applying for a smaller company, it will be important that your personality fits well with those already working in that office. I worked in an office of six employees where everyone was friendly, but when it came to work, everyone was so focused that the office stayed pretty quiet. We decided to hire a new person into the office and though her qualifications for the position were applicable, we soon came to find out that this new hire was a chatterbox. Every day she would share personal stories from home or talk about a work situation that she either found humorous or annoying. Even though we would have freely listened to her in a different environment, the office setting was too fast paced and busy for anyone to return the conversation. In fact, it would often just distract from the sense of urgency that needed to be a part of the business day. It is so important for companies to find that perfect fit, so they can move the goals of the company forward quickly and efficiently. A cover letter can provide the small insight needed to assure the company that you are that perfect fit.

Another reason employers like to see a cover letter is that it gives the whole hiring process a touch of humanity. Reading resume after resume can become exhausting, but a fresh cover letter brings life from the page. Instead of looking at a page of words, the employer can look at reflections of the candidates' minds.

Impress Them with Your Wit

When I first met my husband, I decided to read up and study everything I could about his craft: motocross. I looked up everything from different race teams to how to build a motor for the bike, and on each date had a new piece of information to throw out and blow his mind. It worked…we're married.

In the same way, impress your potential employers. Your cover letter should touch on one or two things the company has accomplished, or praise the way their operation works. Show your interest in the company, not just the job position. Employers want to hire someone that is invested in the company and who isn't just looking for the next paycheck. Let them know that your interests align with the company's ambitions. Show that by choosing you, the company can grow while investing in a successful future.

Be Charming

While putting all the right pieces together for your cover letter, top it off with some charisma. Win your reader over with your charm. If you have a humorously sarcastic personality, write something that will make your reader smile. If you have a gentle spirit, appeal to the reader's compassionate side. Keep your audience in mind as well as the fact that your reader will have many letters and resumes to go through. Strive to put an abundance of quality in a small quantity of words.

Chapter Four
REFERENCES – IN OTHERS' WORDS

***

Building a strong network of references is essential for the hiring process. Prospective employers often call the references that are provided to get a better outside prospective of the applicant's work ethic and personality. I've known a supervisor to weigh the decision of hiring an applicant heavily on the conversations with the references.

Of course, no one is going to list a reference that has a negative assessment of their work abilities and attitude, but it reflects better to have shining references from people who enjoyed working with you and who would love to see you succeed in anything you did.

To obtain this list of shining references, there are a few things to consider:

1. BE PROUD

Know that you are blessed to be working -- with the unemployment rates in this country consistently high, know that having employment warrants gratefulness. Be proud that you are able to contribute back to society by holding a job of ANY kind. From mopping floors to owning a Forbes noteworthy business, every position should be held with honor and executed with a sense of pride. All jobs are a part of a larger picture, creating a well-oiled machine that allows the overall purpose to be accomplished. No job is unremarkable, and ALL jobs are required (else there wouldn't be an opening for such a position). As you work with this mindset, your pride will reflect in your effort and people will take notice.

2. BE KNOWN

Even if it isn't in your original make-up to socialize, make an effort to introduce yourself to all supervisors and co-workers. Know the people who you work with daily, and make it a point to converse with them, even if it is only to say hello. Use their names and make them remember yours.

The more who know who you are, the more of an overall impression you'll make with the company. Anytime you have a chance to meet or see a supervisor, shake their hands and make it a point to look them in the eye. Make people remember you in a pleasant and welcoming way.

3. BE PRESENT

When at work, be present at work. There are all sorts of outside variables that we all have to deal with daily. Try not to bring all the outside drama to work. Though you may become comfortable enough with your co-workers to talk with them about what is going on outside of work, no one likes the 'chatty-Cathy' who continues to dump their stories while others are trying to get work done. Show that your priority is the company.

Chapter Five
OKAY, SO YOU LOOK GOOD ON PAPER, NOW SHOW YOUR FACE

***

You've landed the interview—what's next? Since you've already put together an impressive resume, you want to make sure that you are equally as striking when the employers meet you in person. Yes, the field of applicants has narrowed, but at this stage, employers are still hoping to find that one person that stands out above the rest to welcome to their company.

Everything matters in the interview. From your first handshake to the minute you step out the door of the office, you are being watched and evaluated. Always be on your game, be aware of how you are speaking, your body language and facial expressions. Be aware of your grammar as well as your answers to each question. Don't Fluck It Up!

If the Shoe Fits

Attire is extremely important when heading to an interview. You always want to be professional, but you also have to gauge your attire by the *type* of job for which you are interviewing.

I once interviewed for a coordination position at a prestigious law firm. I went onto their website and saw that each picture had men dressed in dark suits, white, collared button down shirts, completed with a solid tie. The women were all in dark pant suits or pencil skirts with a matching blazer, worn with a white, collared button down shirt and closed-toed heels. I assessed that they were looking for someone who fit the part, dressed conservatively, and was there to work hard. My dress of choice was a black, knee-length skirt with a white, collared button down shirt, nude pantyhose (yes, those are still around) and black closed-toed heels. My hair was worn in a neat ponytail. I did not own a suit, but I was still able to dress in a similar fashion.

The interview went well, and I was called back the same day as a finalist for the position. I don't attribute that to the attire only, but it sure made the correct visual impression on my potential employer.

Determine the atmosphere of the interview you are going into. It is important to be a visual fit just as much as being a skillful fit. The company's website is usually a great tool to determine the dress code, not only from the people pictured on the site, but even the language on the website.

Be aware of your overall look. Your look can say a lot about your personality. Wearing more color can denote a bright and colorful personality, or confident demeanor, while wearing strictly black and white can imply a strictly business-minded attitude.

I'm a firm believer in the golden rule of assumptions: To ASSUME makes an ASS out of U and ME, but as much as we'd like to think or believe otherwise, we live in a world of visual judgment and critique. The workplace is no exception. Though profiling and discrimination are often illegal in the hiring process, there are subconscious assumptions that could be made by looking at attire and accessories.

In my office, I sit next to a window that opens to the parking lot. One of the first things I notice when candidates come in for an interview is what type of vehicle they drive. If the car is flashy and new, but the candidate is pretty young, I can assume a few things:

1. Material commodities and social appearances are of high importance to this candidate hence their money goes towards keeping with the status quo (i.e. motivated by money and status).
2. If the car is clean, you know the candidate takes care of personal items. Keeping a work area clean and organized is important in any work environment.

Next, particularly for ladies, I notice their handbags and shoes. (This is possibly because I'm a fan of window-shopping, even when the shoes are on someone else's feet.) I can come to similar assumptions by looking at these accessories. There is a level of wanting to look your best for the potential employer, but certain unnecessary accessories can be suggestive of materialism.

There are jobs that require people to be up to date on the latest and greatest styles. For example, jobs in fashion or social media require a certain level of appreciation for material assets. In other jobs, however, materialism can advocate a "me" personality, when the employer will likely be looking for a "we" attitude.

I am not claiming that bringing your best designer purse or driving your fancy wheels will hinder your chances. I'm only suggesting that in the world of immediate assessment and judgment in which we live, those are things that speak about your person.

From the Tip Jar

Here are a few things to keep in mind when preparing for the interview:
- Always dress professionally, even if the job is more casual in nature
- Men should always start with black/brown slacks, button down shirt, and dress shoes. Depending on dress code, men can add a tie and/or blazer. If the position calls for it, men can dress up to a full suit.

• Men-wear a belt. You don't want to be caught with your pants down (pun intended).

• Women should never wear any dress or skirt that comes above the knee.

• Women-cover up the cleavage. We've come so far to promote equality in the workplace, and using your sexuality to land you a job is only conforming back to old chauvinistic ways.

• Don't cake on the make-up. Let the make-up enhance your already beautiful face by wearing neutral colors.

• Be careful of over accessorizing your outfits. Keep your outfit simple and let your personality shine more than your jewelry.

• Keep your hair out of your face. You don't want to be messing with your hair throughout the interview.

• Do not soak yourself in perfume or cologne. A light scent is okay, but make sure it is a neutral scent and not overbearing-stay away from anything fruity.

• Do not chew gum in the interview.

• Have fresh breath for the interview; you'll be speaking most of the time so you don't want to worry about having foul breath.

• Turn off your cell phone. You don't want any distractions or interruptions when you're interviewing.

• Smile. Employers want to know you are enthusiastic and excited to be there. In the words of the Broadway musical, *Annie,* 'You're never fully dressed without a smile!'

Research and Investigate

Now it's crunch time. Usually, when invited in for an interview, you have only a short couple of days to prepare. Even so, there are some key ways to get ready. One thing to keep in mind is that this interview is not just one sided. You are also there to make sure you want to accept the company as your employer. Provide yourself with all the necessary tools to make an educated decision.

Go online and research the company. Know some of their main achievements, and fundamental objectives. Understand what the company takes pride in as well as their philosophies behind their operation. Next, search the company on the Internet to see if it has been in the news recently. You'll want to take out the notepad and highlighter to help with your studying so you can conversationally allude to what you know about the company. Pick up on some of the vocabulary used in the company's line of business and, if comfortable, slip it into one of your interview answers.

It is also important to know about the nature of the business. Know the company's largest competitors as well as basic governmental decisions that have, or will, affect the industry. Being prepared and informed about the company and industry will allow for a more in depth interview and will also impress your potential employer, confirming your interest in the position.

Once you feel comfortable with background information about the company, research the type of candidate they are looking for to fill the open position. Reread the job description and pick out the key descriptive words embedded within. Keep those attributes in mind when answering questions or giving examples. Use those words specifically in your interview as the potential employer is looking to pick up on them as a match. Be aware of the fine line between using key words from the job description to help focus on your strengths and simply reiterating them. The interview is not a test of memory, but a chance to verbalize how you embody the adjectives that align with the position.

Obviously, you chose to send in your application for this position because you knew you could contribute a specific set of skills to the company. Be comfortable and confident in your accomplishments and knowledge, making sure to highlight them in your interview.

Preparation and Practice

Each employer is calling you in to see how you will answer a series of questions they've created for their hiring process. You might be asked some pretty generic questions, but an invested employer will always compile some questions surrounding *your* particular resume.

Make sure you are prepared to elegantly and honestly answer any questions the employers might have for you. Practice interviewing with a friend and have them think of different questions that put you on the spot. The interview process can be a nerve-racking one, especially when you are unprepared; and though the interviewer knows you are human and can see that you are nervous, there is nothing more unattractive to a future employer than someone who either takes too long to think of an answer, or responds with a colorless, "ummmm…." On the other hand, you don't want to look over rehearsed and mundane.

Know that there are many other candidates who are being asked the same questions. You do not want to have the same answers as another candidate. Even though there are numerous articles and guides on how to answer interview questions, stray away from letting another source answer your questions. You want to make sure that there is an essence of yourself in every answer you give--an *authenticity*.

One young man I interviewed for a customer service focused position seemed to have great qualifications on his resume, but throughout the interview he answered with a monotone voice. There were even moments when we sat in silence waiting for him to think of his answer. Unacceptable.

Though you can never be sure what questions you will be asked there are a few that always seem to show up in an interview. The potential employers are not only looking for how you handle yourself under pressure, but they are also looking to get to know you. Even though you should keep some of those key words in your head from the position description, be honest in answering your questions. If the position is not a great fit, you will be putting yourself and the company in an awkward and unproductive position.

Listen to the interviewer and focus on what type of work environment you will be working in if you are offered the job. This is not just a time for you to be interrogated, but for you to make sure that you *want* the job. It's okay if you end up NOT wanting that particular job.

* * *

Most Frequently Asked Questions:

1. Why do you want to work in this position?

Everyone who applies for the position believes that they are the best candidate for the company. Employers want to know that their employees are excited to be a part of their team. They want your answer to be enthusiastic and fairly detailed. You should try to answer with reasons the job interests you, what you can bring to the position, and what you respect or find interesting about the company itself.

Win the employer over with your eagerness to get involved in the company's vision.

Ex: This position seems active and engaging. I believe it will allow me to utilize and improve my love of customer service. I was also impressed with the amount of care the company puts into harvesting its own coffee beans from many exotic origins. I'd like to learn more about where they come from and how they're made.

2. What are your three best qualities or strengths?

The employer wants to hear what you can bring to their company dynamics. You should know your best qualities and how they will promote success in the workplace. Your answer can be short and sweet, while giving a brief explanation for each quality.

Ex: I pride myself in being loyal to a company and its cause(s), striving to further embrace the company's goals by making them my own. I am a quick and enthusiastic learner. Not only can I learn new tasks and routines quickly, but I also invite the opportunity to learn continuously and take on more responsibility. Finally, I am a team player. I believe that in order for a team to succeed, all players need to be focused on the large picture rather than an individual feat.

3. What are your three worst qualities or weaknesses?

There are a couple reasons this question is asked frequently. Many times it can throw you off your game to think of things that you do not necessarily do well. You probably don't dwell on things you *cannot* do well, particularly when you are trying to move your life forward. Even if you know your weaknesses, they generally are not things you'd want to share with a possible employer. Another reason employers may ask this question is to see if you know where you can improve. Knowing your own weaknesses is strength in itself because you can also be aware of how to compensate for them. Your answer should be humble, though optimistic. You should offer an answer that includes how you have already addressed your weaknesses and turned them into strengths.

Ex: I can be a bit of a work-o-holic because I don't like leaving things undone, though I've picked up a few hobbies to separate work and home life. I get frustrated when I don't know what I'm doing, but I'm not afraid to ask questions to understand, and am persistent when it comes to taking notes and learning the task. I don't operate well when being micromanaged, which is why I take so much pride in my work, so others will know that I'm as detailed and serious as they are about the company.

4. What are your long-term career goals?

Employers want to know that they are investing in you as an employee. They want to know that you will be happy to make this company a part of your long-term career, and/or that the skills you hope to gain from the position will move you towards your larger goals. You can be honest about what you want to do in life, but if your answer is not to be at the company for a long time, then make sure you highlight why you believe the position is a great stepping stone for your career path.

Ex: Eventually, I'd like to work as a designer for a large apparel company. I plan to get my degree in fashion merchandising, but would like to learn about the fashion basics and gain experience in all departments of making a recognizable brand. I believe managing this store would provide valuable knowledge to move forward in this industry.

**5. Why are you looking to leave your current job? /
Why did you leave your last job?**

My general advice is to answer each question honestly and
with this one in particular, it is important to be sure your
facts are accurate. The interviewer can easily call your
previous employer to check your reasons for leaving to find
out whether your leave was amicable or not. Be honest
about why you are interviewing, whether it be that you
were laid off from your last position, are looking for a new
career, or that you really did not feel your previous position
was right for you.

*Ex: In my current position, I've reached a plateau and
there are no opportunities to move up in the company. I'd
like to find a job where my skills are most effectively used
and I continue to be challenged.*

6. What's your ideal work environment?

This question is to make sure that you will be comfortable
working in the environment that the position provides.
Think about your perfect workplace: How many people do
you work with? How much responsibility do you share
with others? Do you like a workplace where your fellow
employees are conversational, or do you like it quieter? Do

you like to be on the phone, or would you rather bury your head in physical work? These are all questions to consider regarding your work surroundings. Your answer will tell an employer what your particular needs and preferences are in order to help you succeed. It can also give the employer an idea of what might be a distraction for you.

Ex: I enjoy a workplace that is constantly busy and always changing. I get bored with situations that are too redundant or mundane. I thrive in high-stress environments and find that I work extremely well when given independent responsibilities. I enjoy interacting with clients and creating relationships.

7. What motivates you?

The employer wants to make sure that they are hiring someone who will excitedly rise to the challenges of the position. They want to know what continues to make you get up for work every morning, or what pushes you to work harder. This motivation is different for everyone. For example, if you are the head of the household, your motivation might be to provide for your family, or be able to spend your time off with your children. For others, money might be motivation enough. Whatever drives you to do your best is going to be your best answer. Make sure to shape your answer with care and reason.

Ex: Being able to help others motivates me. I flourish in an environment where my hard work can bring joy to someone else, or where I know I am making a difference in someone's life. Hearing others' excitement and appreciation only pushes me to provide that same feeling for more people.

8. What's your biggest pet peeve in the workplace?

This is another question about work environment. The employer wants to be sure that you fit well in the office surroundings. This question is meant to pick up on what you do not like in the workplace, which can also shed a little light on your preferred work environment.

Ex: My biggest pet peeve in the workplace is when people don't follow through. I like to be able to work in a trusting environment where I don't constantly have to make sure that responsibilities, other than my own, are getting done. I believe that a workplace is a team environment, and when one person fails to complete their part of the work then it reflects poorly on the entire team.

9. If you were any animal, which one would you be and why?

This is my most favorite question I've ever been asked in an interview. It was absolutely meant to throw me off and make me think quickly on my toes, while peeking into my creativity and playfulness. You might encounter some goofier questions like this not only to end the interview on a lighter note, but also to test your creativity. Have fun with these questions, but be ready to give an answer. You do not want to sit there in silence thinking of an answer. If you can't come up with a clever answer on the spot, take a stab at it and smile afterwards.

Ex: I'd definitely be a velociraptor because even though they are small, they are smart, fast, and determined to get what they want.

Guaranteed Impression: Last Question

One thing that can guarantee a good impression on your potential employer is to come prepared to ask questions about the company to see if they are a fit for you. If nothing else in the interview goes well, at least have your prepared questions ready to go to turn the interview around, leaving a positive impression on your interviewer.

Do you have any questions for me?

YES. The answer to this question should always be, "yes." In fact, it is best to prepare a list of 10-15 thoughtful questions for the employer, typed and neatly placed in your folder or portfolio. This lets the employer know that you are serious about the position and that you want to know more about the job and company. It is a way for you to take some control during the interview and turn questions around. *Is this company what I'm looking for?*

Ask questions about advancement opportunities, pros and cons of the position, and even why the company is looking to hire. Ask about your interviewer's favorite aspect of working with the company. These are important things for you to know as a potential employee.

Once you have all the logistical questions done, use the research you did previously on the company to ask about recent accomplishments or setbacks. Ask how competitive they are in their field. You may also want to know things about the company that are more relevant to your personal life, such as their efforts to be environmentally friendly, etc. Engage your interviewer in intelligent banter and force them to take a look at the core ideals of the company.

Example Questions:

- *Why has this position become available?*
You'll want to be aware of why the company is in need of a new hire for this position. In some cases, the company might have created this new position to fulfill a need, but in others, you might find that the previous employee in that position was either fired or quit. If that's the case, you might want to inquire why that happened. Most companies will not say anything inappropriate about a previous employee, but they might give you hints about why that particular person didn't want that position anymore.

- *Is there room to grow within the company?*
Understand the type of company for which you're interviewing. In smaller companies, there is less room for advancement, which may or may not coincide with your personal career goals. In smaller companies, however, all positions are essential to the running of the company. Likewise, in larger companies, there may be more room for

advancement, but certain positions could be more expendable should the company have to make budget cuts.

- ***What are some of the biggest stressors and rewards of this position?***

Understanding the type of stressors you'll face throughout your workday is a huge help to dealing with them in a healthy way. Asking about these stressors and rewards upfront will allow you to measure if the stress load is manageable for you, as well as if the rewards are enough to motivate you.

- ***What's your favorite part about working here?***

Your interviewer might be caught a bit off guard with this question, but if they genuinely enjoy working with the company, they will have an easy time answering. It is important to know if your potential co-workers enjoy their work environment. You also want to know that your interviewer can pick from many things that they love about working with the company.

- *I noticed that your company was recently in the news as being one of the top in the industry. How does this company plan to continue that reputation and maintain a top industry leader?*

Create thoughtful questions that challenge your interviewer. Let them know you've done your research about them and are very interested in being a part of the company. You'll find that interviewers are impressed and appreciate the simple fact that you've put effort into your time with them. If you've researched the company and found that they've had negative attention in the news, don't be afraid to bring that up and ask about how they're handling the media as well as correcting the potential problems.

One of my previous employers used to brag to his friends and clients about the questions I brought to my interview. He said he was taken aback at first, and even a bit intimidated, but was so impressed with my preparation that he knew I was the right choice for the job even though I had no experience in the field.

Asking questions to end the interview leaves a lasting impression, especially if the questions are thoughtful and evoke more conversation. It demonstrates your preparedness and professionalism.

When I had a chance to interview potential hires, it would really bother me if someone did not have any questions for me. I felt as though I had read their resume, come up with thoughtful questions for them to present themselves further, invited them to talk with me, and that time and work I allotted for their visit was not reciprocated. It was a deciding factor for me: no questions for me, not getting hired. Sounds harsh, but if the potential hire is not willing to put in a small amount of work and time to prepare to meet with me, then I cannot assume that they will go above and beyond what is expected in the actual position.

Pay Day

What is your expected salary range? Some companies will ask what your desired salary is. This is loaded question. Companies, especially in this economy, are looking to cut budget any way possible, but do not want to miss out on the chance to hire an exceptional employee. If your salary range is too high, the company might not have the flexibility in their budget to hire you, but if your range is too low, you could be cheating yourself out of proper payment for the position. It is best to come with a number that is still fair for the position, but sits at the higher end of your salary range. Let the company and hiring manager know that you are willing to negotiate on that number, but feel it is a reasonable assessment for the position.

Before I knew how to correctly answer this question, I had answered it fairly conservatively in an interview with an event company. The title was one that suggested a higher rank within the company, which I assumed would be rewarded with higher pay. When the position was offered to me, it was submitted with my lowest ranged salary. I was happy to take the position, but felt that I had been cheated out of a higher pay range. You can bet that I asked for a healthy raise after the first year of proving my talents and commitment to the company.

It's Okay Not to Know

When you're asked a question that you don't know the answer to, say "I don't know," rather than trying to fake an answer on the spot which might put you into an embarrassing situation. The interviewer might ask questions to get a feel for your knowledge of the company and it is okay not to know everything. To counter your lack of knowledge, show interest in the subject. Ask about that particular component of the company. Instead of impressing them with your knowledge, you can impress them with your eagerness and willingness to learn more about how the company works.

Side note: You do not want to answer "I don't know" to questions pertaining to yourself and your experience. Be confident in your answers about yourself to show that you've taken the time to do some self-assessment and you know the type of worker you are as well as the type of work environment you thrive in.

Chapter Six
PRACTICE MAKES PERFECT

***

When I was in school, I took a public speaking class where we had to stand in front of the class and give a five-minute persuasive presentation on a controversial subject. I thought I was prepared enough and that I had enough evidence to persuade my classmates' opinions to align with my own. I had pictures, a heartbreaking story and shocking statistics, but failed to practice before I presented. I figured the subject was shocking enough that I would be able to fill my allotted time with all the information I had found and would just wing the rest of the presentation. I ended up with a presentation of about three minutes, blank stares on my classmates' faces and a less compelling argument than I thought I had. Needless to say, it wasn't my finest moment.

As with any performance or competition, you want to make sure your craft is rehearsed before you are in the spotlight with all eyes on you. You want to deliver a flawless performance, showing that you are prepared and confident. The interviewer is sitting through a few interviews per day, asking the same questions multiple times, and most likely getting many of the same answers. Be that refreshing breath of air that captures their attention from the beginning with your confident smile, firm handshake and appropriate outfit. Then, make them remember you with your convincing answers and captivating personality.

Someone Else's Story

You don't want to be the broken record that the hiring manager has heard too many times before. Try to imagine what the most popular answer might be, then improve on it, or change your answer altogether. Sometimes, the common answers are popular because they are acceptable and agreeable. However, if common answers become too favored by potential hires, then it can appear that the interviewees took the easy way out. Not only will the interviewer have heard the same answers before, but they will be bored with your robotic answers as well as turned off by the lack of creativity. If the open position has opportunities for advancement or managerial elements, the company is most likely looking for a person with leadership qualities who will think and speak for themselves.

Try to give intelligent answers that reflect your preparedness for the interview. There is a difference between sounding rehearsed and sounding prepared so practice with a friend, family member, or even in the mirror. Practice until you are comfortable with your answers.

Mirror, Mirror

I'm an avid mirror-talker. I like to sit in front of my own reflection and see what I look like when I make different expressions or reactions. Often when putting on makeup in the mornings, my husband will catch me playing with my expressions or talking to myself about nothing at all (and sometimes in different accents). Become comfortable with yourself and know what you look like, and how you sound. Work on your voice inflection and volume. Be goofy with your reflection, even if others are watching. The more comfortable you become in your own awkwardness, the more comfortable you'll be in other environments and situations.

If you are struggling with talking to yourself in the mirror to study your expressions and reactions, try starting with something a bit simpler. Put on your favorite song and lip sync along. Pretend you are performing on stage in front of a huge crowd and let them know you're passionate about the lyrics. It's okay to be goofy—in fact, it's recommended! Again, become comfortable in your own skin, building confidence that will emote throughout your interviews.

It sounds like a lot to think about for a little interview, but the following exercises will help you beyond the workplace. They will help you to be more assertive and confident in business and personal relationships.

Expression

When I was very young, my dad would play a game with my sisters and me called 'faces.' He would yell out an expression and we'd have to make that face. "Happy Face!" and we'd plaster the biggest smiles on our faces showing every one of our teeth. "Angry Face!" and we'd furrow our brows, scrunch our noses and purse our lips while tucking our chins down to our chests.

Though it was a child's game helping us to develop and express our emotions, the game is wonderful when practicing for interviews. Given your actual expressions and reactions will be more subtle, the same idea stands. Watch to see how you react to information, whether it is exciting or cautionary. You might be amazed at how your reactions do not come across in regular conversation as much as you think they do (or, contrary wise, come across too strong). I have interviewed so many people who seemed like they were just staring right through me the entire time. They looked completely vacant; though I'm sure they thought they were engaging in the conversation. Remember that a blank face or minimal facial expressions can read as bored or uninterested. Who wants to hire someone that isn't interested or passionate about the position and company?

Voice Inflection, Volume and Pronunciation

It is so important to be heard. Not only should you speak up, but you also want to articulate your words so that you can be perfectly understood. We've all experienced trying to talk with someone that mumbles his or her words. Either you are stuck asking 'what?' after each statement, or you give up and nod, pretending like you know what is being said, looking for a way out of the conversation. Along with being aware of your expression, you want to consciously adjust your vocal inflection.

I have endured many interviewees who spoke in such dreadful monotone it bored me to hear their answers. Particularly, the position I was looking to hire for was one with a high level of customer service. There was no way I would allow anyone who spoke in a monotone during the interview to talk to my clients. I'd lose business!

As you focus on your voice inflection, play with the different levels of your voice. Of course, you won't want to fluctuate too much when being interviewed, sounding like a child's cartoon, but you certainly do not want to stay at one even tone the entire time. By playing with the levels of inflection in your voice, you will be able to place emphasis on the important points you want to make within your interview while letting your interviewer know that you are involved in the conversation.

Volume and inflection go hand in hand. In regular conversation, you will notice that more often than not, we tend to drop the ends of our sentences. We were taught in grade school that when we come to the end of a sentence we drop our voices to signify the period. The problem with this rule in interviews is that oftentimes, we'll mumble the ends of our sentences, making our sentence conclusion unclear. Likewise, we were taught to raise our vocal pitch when asking questions to denote the question mark.

Now to shake up everything you've learned---try to raise your pitch slightly when coming to the end of a sentence and speak out.

This doesn't mean to make the sentence into a question, but rather ditch the mumbled ending as follows:

I   worked there   for   four   years.

You can still present an end to your statement, but this way, the end of your answer will not be lost. This is a great exercise to practice either with a friend or by recording yourself. Find any magazine, book or pamphlet, and read a page while trying to raise your pitch to create a strong finish to your sentences. You'll be able to hear a clear difference.

Nervous Ticks

Everyone has his or her own nervous ticks. A nervous tick is anything that you do subconsciously to keep your nerves at bay or to stay focused. The only downfall is that these ticks are repeated physical actions that clearly signify that the nerves are present. Sometimes we develop these ticks to delay answering or to find the right words to say, but it only distracts from your actual answers.

My own nervous tick was throwing in "uhh" in my sentences. At first, I had no idea how many times I would interrupt my idea. After recording myself, I was surprised at how unpleasant that sound would make my answers. Instead of hearing what I was saying on the recording, I was distracted by how many times the "uhh" came into my speech. My problem was that my brain worked much faster than I could speak, and I would either end up stumbling over my words, or creating a space to slow down and articulate. To remedy this tick, I worked on slowing down my answers, consciously choosing my words and avoiding any space fillers.

Other common ticks include things like clearing your throat before each answer, constantly playing with your hair, certain repeated hand gestures, space fillers ("umm"/"uhh"), leg bouncing, touching your face, rubbing your hands on your legs, and many more. Be aware of these types of ticks in yourself that may distract from your interview.

The Minute You Walk Through the Door

The minute you open that office door, the interview has begun (and a quick hint - that designated minute better be before the scheduled time for the interview). 'Being on time' means that you are checking in with the receptionist about five to ten minutes prior to your allotted interview appointment. This shows characteristics of time management and responsibility. Don't let your interviewer wait on you. To be on time, there are a few things to consider when preparing for your interview: Set your alarm to wake you nice and early so you have time to get ready and double check all your interview supplies. Look up the directions to the interviewer's office the night before. Check the traffic report to allow for enough driving time.

Let's face it. Life happens. If something happens that puts you behind schedule to the point where you know you won't make the interview on time, call ahead and quickly explain your situation and location. It is better that your interviewer knows you are going to be later than expected than to think you are just bad with time management.

Be cordial with anyone at the reception desk, be pleasant, and even smile at anyone who happens to walk by while you wait to be interviewed. You never know who your immediate supervisor will be once you get the job, so it's better to start work relationships in a very professional manner. One of my bosses made sure to be in his office with the door closed when the candidates would come in to interview. He would have me sit at the front desk and get a feel for the person while they were waiting for him. Little did they know they were already being interviewed and examined by me. I look much younger than my age, which made me less threatening to engage in a conversation. No one suspected that I had any say in the hiring process.

One woman that was coming to interview was told that she would be speaking with my boss, a man. She arrived dressed in tight, revealing clothing, hair teased and curled, and thick red lipstick. She walked up to me and asked me to "let him know I'm here, hun." I couldn't believe it. She then proceeded to fluff her hair and position her…assets…while waiting for my boss. It sounds like something out of a bad movie, but, alas, I've seen it all. Needless to say, she did not get the job.

If you get that position, you're going to be working closely with all the employees in the office. You'll be spending so much time with these people, and they all deserve your upmost respect. Every one of those employees will have a different personality. There are different personality types that are wonderfully suited for specific jobs and your success will be, in part, how you can thrive while working with ALL types of personalities. If nothing else, show your (future) co-workers respect as you are all working towards a common goal.

Let Me Hear Your Body Talk

Even if the words from your mouth are intelligent and absorbing, what is your body language saying? With the wrong body language, you could be sending opposing messages to your interviewer.

I was interviewing a candidate who was perfect on paper and even showed up to the interview dressed to impress. He successfully engaged me with his answers, and impressed me with his knowledge of the company, but there was one thing that hindered his chances of getting the position: his body language. This candidate slouched in the chair, put his foot up on the coffee table, avoided making eye contact and even interrupted my questions to provide his answers. His body language told me he wasn't interested in speaking to me and his know-it-all demeanor came off as rude and arrogant.

He had become too comfortable with the routine of interviewing. He did everything right to prepare himself for the questions of the interview, but forgot to maintain his professional presence. He acted as though I was wasting his time by asking him the same questions that other potential employers had asked him in past interviews. Even if this was the ump-teenth time he interviewed, he should have treated it like his first and only.

Be aware of your body language and stature. Sit up straight, make eye-contact with your interviewer and show them your most professional self while engaging them in conversation. Nod in agreement when listening to the interviewer explain the position and skill requirements and ask questions when you are unsure what they are talking about. Let your body talk just as loudly as your voice.

If this particular candidate had cared to pay attention to my body language, he would have recognized my discomfort with his disposition and my dissipating interest in him as an employee.

Chapter Seven
DON'T FLUCK IT UP

***

Now that you've prepared on all levels, there is one more thing to keep in mind: Don't Fluck it up. Let me explain:

FLUCK = Fluff + Stuck

Often times in conversation, we like to fluff our stories and answers to provide a detailed account for our listeners. We may fancy ourselves great storytellers and entertainers, and thus attempt to become Shakespeare, reciting poetic imagery and detailed metaphors. Though 'fluffing' is a great quality for campfires and get-togethers, it has no place in the job interview. Stick to the subject and answer the interview questions directly. When you start to **fluff** your answers, you will find that you'll get **stuck** in your thoughts and forget what you were talking about, causing you to stray away from the actual question.

Too many details can be confusing and hard to follow. Remember, there is an abundance of applicants the interviewer has to get through and they don't have time to hear lots of fluff. The worst-case scenario, you might even get cut off before getting to the meat of your answer.

One of my supervisors was notorious for cutting off candidates that fluffed their answers. If he detected any straying from his question, he would immediately take control of the conversation and either re-word his question or just move on to the next. I'd watch as he would mark little notes next to the questions after they would be answered (or not answered) so that he could remember the conversation he had with any particular candidate. His primary complaint about potential candidates was that they were too talkative or weren't able to track with his questions.

When you leave an interview, you want the interviewer to remember your answers as solid and concise. Being straightforward with your answers will come across as honest and eager to begin working which are qualities that companies want.

When you practice cutting out all the fluff, do so with a friend, family member, or mentor. This can also be done by tape recording yourself, but what you might think is a valid detail can sound like fluff to an unbiased ear. Have someone ask you questions and stop your answers the minute you start fluffing or going off on a tangent. Experiment with the idea of fluffing and giving detail so you can feel the conversation get stuck, then practice until you feel you can cut the fluff on your own.

My husband is notorious for *flucking up* his stories. He'll come home and want to tell me about one event that happened in his day, but will start from the minute he woke up. Half the time, I don't even get to hear about the actual event that he began talking about because he took the conversation on a rollercoaster of tangents. I find myself having to track his conversation more intently than with others so that when he asks me "What was I saying?" or

"Wait, what were we just talking about?" I can be there with the save.

I don't want details about how he brushed his teeth after putting on his slippers unless it's relevant to his story. If he begins his story with irrelevant facts, I find myself interrupting and restarting the story closer to the point: "Okay, okay – so then you got to work...and..." This is fine for home conversations, and great for sitting around the campfire, but it would be nerve-racking to have a potential employer cut you off and hurry your answer along.

The less detailed your answers are, the smaller the chance of you straying from the question. This doesn't mean that the employer won't want any detail, but try to stick to the specific information they have asked for instead of providing unnecessary proclamations. I might love hearing about my husband's dental history, but your interviewer(s) will not be so interested.

Use Your Yoga – Embrace the Silence

In this crazy generation of constant noise, it can be difficult to allow for silence. Silence can seem awkward and uncomfortable, yet it is a gift to be able to embrace the quietness. In an interview, silence from the interviewer does not signify that they are unhappy with your answer, or that they are waiting for you to continue with a lengthier explanation. Silence often occurs when the interviewer is simply finishing notes from your answer and preparing their next question.

I interviewed a young lady for an administrative position and though her answers were competent, it was more than obvious that my silence between questions was making her uncomfortable. If I was not ready with the next question right away, she would either continue her last answer, which led her on such a tangent that she forgot what she was talking about in the first place, or she'd start a new topic by compliment me on something I was wearing. I was flattered, but her discomfort was making me anxious. I felt like I needed to rush the interview and thus was unable to get a real feel for the person behind all the jabber.

Use those yoga classes, or find some time to meditate by yourself, even if that means sitting in silence for a few minutes at a time. Sit comfortably in the silence. Think of the silence in an interview as a small break between questions. Show confidence in yourself by taking a breath, sit back and smile while waiting for your interviewer to continue.

Chapter Eight
MASQUERADE – THE PHONE INTERVIEW

***

I have never been a fan of the phone interview. It doesn't matter which side of the conversation I'm on, I don't feel like I can get a sufficient idea of the person on the other end.

Seeing beyond the mask of the phone

When you are offered the dreaded phone interview, let the company know you would be more than happy to schedule a face-to-face meeting with the interviewer and give them your schedule. Sometimes, the situation is set up specifically to interview over the phone. In those cases, you have to win the interview by using only your voice. You have no physical interaction, no body language, no eye contact--all you can use is the inflection of your voice to get your points across, disallowing some of the advantages that could help you stand out otherwise. Beyond that, you also have to deal with the unpredictable (and inevitable) services of the phone companies: dropped calls, bad or no reception, static, and volume difficulties.

I was interviewed over the phone for one position, even though I insisted I wouldn't mind coming in for an in-person interview. The company had an interview system where the applicant was first given a screening interview over the phone, then advanced to a phone interview with the Vice President of the company, and once the group of applicants was narrowed, they would begin calling people to come in for a third interview. It wasn't my favorite scenario, but it was the hand I was dealt in this situation. I still did my homework in researching the company and prepared my questions for the interviewer. I even cleared space in my day to be sure I didn't miss the phone call. As fate would have it, I'm a fairly practical person and the upgrading of my cellular device from my trusty flip-phone was unnecessary, though that often came with the dreaded dropped calls and horrible reception, so I wanted to be sure that I was in a full-bar area that was quiet enough for me to hear the interview questions and answer cleverly.

Being prepared as best I could for the uncontrollable variables, I picked up the call for the screening interview. It was a fairly short and pleasant conversation; though I'm sure I had to ask the interviewer to repeat the questions a couple of times. I felt that I had to overcompensate with my vocal inflection and witty comments since I could not show my interest in any other way. I had to make sure the conversation was comfortable enough that the screening would successfully push me forward to the next interview. Done.

For the second interview, my phone decided that it wanted to take a day off. I could not find a place that would give me full reception (come to find out, the cell phone towers in my area were down that day). The call dropped twice and I had to wait for a call back from the Vice President as he was calling from a blocked number, apologizing each time we reconnected. It made for a choppy conversation to say the least. I tried to jump on any piece of information that the VP gave to me to engage in the conversation and make it pleasant, but was unable to get a word in half the time. It becomes a war trying to battle for talking space. I was called for the third interview, but I felt it was by the grace of God--_not_ from the phone interview.

The best thing one can do when asked to do a phone interview is to practice your vocal inflection more than anything else. If it helps, sit in front of the mirror while interviewing over the phone. Your facial expressions will aide your vocal inflection. Fluctuate your tone so as not to sound monotone and boring. Without any tools, other than speaking and listening, it can be hard to portray emotions genuinely.

As I mentioned before, I felt I was overcompensating with my voice to stand out from the other applicants. To me, this didn't seem genuine and the whole point of an interview is to get an honest understanding of the candidate. I also felt that I did not get a real feel for the interviewer. It is so important to have a perception of your potential supervisors and co-workers. With a phone interview, you aren't able to assess the environment that you would be working in with this potential position. How could you know if the environment, people and position are best for you and your personality?

Chapter Nine
FINISH AND FOLLOW UP

***

After all of the nervousness, preparing, questions and impressions, you can finally relax in knowing that you're done with the hard part.

Give a strong handshake

You've made it through the interview. After you end the interview with a firm handshake, you can let out a deep breath, pat yourself on the back and head home knowing you put 100% into the interview. You'll be able to gauge how the interview went by the time you walk out.

A few things that can signify that your interview went well:

- The interview lasted more than fifteen minutes. If the answers you provided sparked a bit of interest and conversation from the interviewer, you'll know that you were able to reach a more personal level of interviewing than just a simple question/answer session.
- You were able to catch a look of pleasant surprise from the interviewer's face.
- You were asked about your availability for a second interview or how much notice you would need to give your current job if offered the position.

These points do not guarantee that you landed the position, but they are good indicators that you are in the running and being seriously considered among the top candidates.

If you feel as though the interview went poorly, remember that we are all human and we all make mistakes. The attitude that separates the successful candidates from the pack is one that will learn from those mistakes to make the next interview better.

Follow up

You thought you were done, but there's one more step to the interview. Because there are so many candidates applying for the same position, you want to stand out as much as possible. Send a thank you email to the interviewer the same day you were interviewed. Do not wait, as it will seem like an afterthought. Writing a thank you to the employer not only shows respect and appreciation for taking time out of their busy workday to consider you, but it also leaves a lasting impression of good manners.

Every Christmas and birthday, after opening all our presents, my mom would have us make a list of what we were given from our friends and relatives. She would then have us write thank you notes to each person to describe our joy and gratefulness. As the years passed, it became second nature to write thank you notes detailed with appreciation. I am always surprised with the warm reaction these simple notes get in return. Everyone wants to feel valued and appreciated.

The same idea goes for the potential employer. It is so nice to hear that your time and efforts are valued. The thank you note can be short, but personalized enough to leave one more impression on the employer. You can reference something that was said in the interview, or touch on something the interviewer might have emphasized. This act of appreciation and kindness will no doubt surface in the decision making process.

Chapter Ten
INTEGRITY OF THE INTERVIEW

***

This book has provided many ways to strengthen your interviewing skills as well as your social and business interaction techniques. By practicing the art of interviewing, you can become a well-spoken candidate for any position. As emphasized many times throughout this instructional, there are going to be positions that will not fit your specific skill set or personality. The ultimate purpose of the interview is for a company to find a candidate that fits, as well as a candidate to find a company that fits. Keep the integrity of the interview by using it as a device for finding this match. Do not accept a position in which you will not excel or contribute. If you are unsure whether your skill set and personality would be a good fit in the position, it might behoove you to ask to shadow the position for a day or two so you can get the general feel of the environment before going through all the new hire paperwork and training.

When I was searching for employment, I found that it was addictive to be contacted for interviews. It was exciting to know that people were interested in what I had to offer and that my resume stood out over many others. If you provide a strong resume and cover letter to the companies you apply for, then you might be getting interviews from all angles, and all at the same time. Make sure this doesn't turn into a game for you.

Every company is on their own time schedule, so even though you might get a few interviews right away, you might get more offers when you least expect them. One thing every company has in common, though, is that they are looking to invest in someone who will stay with the company long term. It is very important to show respect to all employers. I know you cannot control the timing of being offered a position (or two, or three), but be sure to act in a respectful and honorable way.

I recently hired a young man who quit after two days. It was interesting to look back on his first day of working with the company and realize that he had no desire to learn the offered position. He seemed bored and under stimulated, but could not complete any tasks that were given to him. He refused to take notes while in training and would take exceptionally long breaks throughout the day. He presented himself completely different than in his interviews.

When he sent his resignation over email, he just said he realized that the position wasn't for him, but then I found out that he had used our company as leverage to gain a healthy promotion with his previous employer. Not only had we wasted our time with this new hire, but we had also spent a lot of money hiring and told all of our other applicants that we had filled the position.

Hiring a new employee is a very expensive process. I spent hours of time sorting through countless resumes, interviewing candidates, scheduling second interviews and all on company time. After the young man accepted the position, we had to do a background check along with all the hire paperwork, and then have a customized computer shipped from our mother company with his particular programs and passwords. After he emailed his resignation in, we had to ship everything back and start from square one again.

Each company has its own particular hiring process, but they all use company time and money to make sure they are hiring a new employee that will be worth the expense. Compromising the integrity of the interview and hiring process can be a significant loss of time and money for companies, and will stain your name for that company. If word travels around (which it usually does), you might have a hard time getting another job when you're ready to move on from your current one.

Once you accept the position in a company, impress them and make them know they made the right choice. Do not continue to 'shop around' in the job market.

There are exceptions, of course, to every situation, but there are also proper ways to handle these exceptions:

Exceptional Scenarios

1. *You accept and commit to a position with a company, but soon after are offered a better position from a different prospective company. What do you do?*

You might want to go to your supervisor and honestly talk about the other position. Let them know that you applied while you were looking for employment, and they just contacted you to offer the position. If the pay is higher, you might be able to negotiate with the current employer for a higher salary. If the position is more desirable and aligned with your personal goals, just say so. Take into consideration what the next stepping stone in your career should be and weigh the pros and cons of each offer against your ideal career situation. Generally, you'll find that employers are people too and will just want what is best for your career.

2. *Due to variables beyond your control, such as family issues or personal obligations, you must resign from the position. What do you do?*

These situations are always tough—though it is not common, sometimes life calls us to drop everything and focus on something completely different. When life happens, privately meet with your supervisor face-to-face to explain the situation. Again, remember that your employer is also human, and will usually be understanding. In some cases, your new employer might be able to work with your situation to keep you as an employee. Talk about different options and let them know you are willing to fight for your position that they so graciously offered to you.

No matter what the exceptional scenario might be, always keep in mind that honesty is the best policy. Show your employers respect by meeting with them in person, discussing the situation and attempting to come to an amicable solution.

Go Get A Job!

There will be times when you will feel as though all the effort you are putting into finding a job is not giving you the desired results.

A friend of mine had me proof read around ten different cover letters and customized resumes for open positions in her area that catered to her specific talents and interests. She submitted them, landed the interviews, and then didn't hear from them for months. Every time she would call to get a status, she got a really vague answer about the company still interviewing candidates.

She finally applied for and was offered a temporary position. Though this was not her ideal career choice, she accepted the offer in order to make her rent. After a couple weeks as a temporary employee, she was contacted by six of the companies asking if she was still interested in their offered position. She was then able to negotiate the pay she wanted and select the position she felt best fit her.

It is more than important not to give up. Continue to interview and submit your resume. Just when you least expect it, you'll be landing the job you really wanted in the first place. If you come to doors that are locked, look for open windows. Be persistent and push forward.

I've given you the same tools that worked well for me. I compiled this instructional based on my experience as both the *interviewee* (even committing some of the no-nos I've written about) as well as my experience as the *interviewer*. I hope you use these tools to your advantage and find that, mixed with some determination and dedication, you'll be able to land the career that best fits you. Find that niche and begin to give back to the world that can offer so much.

***